THE CRAVING

Titles in the series:

DELETE
TIM COLLINS

IN THE STARS
ECHO FREER

KEEPER
ANN EVANS

KILL ORDER
DANIEL BLYTHE

LAST YEAR
IAIN McLAUGHLIN

PARADISE
TIM COLLINS

S/HE
CATHERINE BRUTON

THE CRAVING
CLIFF McNISH

Badger Publishing Limited, Oldmedow Road, Hardwick Industrial Estate, King's Lynn PE30 4JJ

Telephone: 01438 791037

www.badgerlearning.co.uk

THE CRAVING

CLIFF McNISH

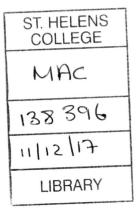
The Craving ISBN 978-1-78464-710-0

Text © Cliff McNish 2017
Complete work © Badger Publishing Limited 2017

Publisher: Susan Ross
Senior Editor: Danny Pearson
Copyediting: Cambridge Publishing Management Ltd
Designer: Bigtop Design Ltd
Cover: A. Astes / Alamy

2 4 6 8 10 9 7 5 3 1

CHAPTER 1
THIRST

It was just after his 15th birthday that Elias began feeling… different.

It started with night sweats and general edginess. Pretty soon he didn't want to be around people much. Then came the thirst – a dry mouth no matter how much water he drank. What was going on?

The weirdest thing was that his parents seemed unconcerned. Even when Elias spent more time isolated in his room, and stopped eating fruit or vegetables any more, they never once suggested he see a doctor.

To take his mind off things, he began taking long walks alone at night. Something about the midnight hours – the darkness? the cold? – drew him out.

Elias had plenty of space to wander. His home and its grounds extended for miles. His parents were rich. His father was a bigwig in some never-spoken-about job. Whatever he did, Elias knew it had to be super important because he'd been wrapped in special protection his whole life: never left for long on his own, home-schooled, his friends chosen carefully. People were always watching him, too. His parents called them 'house servants', but Elias knew they were guards.

Actually, something had happened when Elias was seven years old that made him realise his safety was more important than that of the children of the other families. He'd tripped up on the lawn. It was nothing – just a twist of his ankle during football. But the reaction! Every adult visiting that day had run towards him. They'd forgotten their own children in their rush to get to him.

Home life with his parents and their friends was pretty odd in other ways, too. There were often weird night-time episodes – parties with no drinking, but where the adults seemed to get more and more excited, staying out late while he was minded at home.

*

It was a few days after he started taking night strolls that Elias' first true craving occurred.

He woke to a surprising rasping noise. What made it really surprising was that the noise came from him. His mouth, tongue lapping warmly, was attached to a small cut on his arm. He'd grazed it on a railing earlier that day, and now he was sucking at the wound in his sleep.

Horrified, Elias jumped out of bed. A cooling breeze wafted over his hot face from the window, but it did nothing to stop the panic.

Or the thirst. His entire throat was on fire.

Hurrying to the kitchen, he drank four full glasses of water, but was still parched. What on earth was wrong with him?

Moments later, he was standing beside the open fridge when he caught sight of himself in a side mirror. When was the last time he'd had a decent meal? He was so pale and thin he barely recognised himself. He looked like a gaunt wraith in the moonlight.

Then he caught a whiff from the fridge – a scent attracting him. His nose guided him towards a package at the back of the second shelf.

He carefully unwrapped it. Even before he saw that something wet and heavy was inside, he could smell the blood. A steak waiting to be cooked?

He dropped the package onto the floor when he saw the contents spill out. Inside was what his parents called offal: internal organs. There was a heart, mixed with kidneys and a sloppy white string of intestines.

Elias backed away in horror. He'd wanted to be close to that? Many times he'd seen his mother and father eating offal at lunch and dinner, but he'd never wanted to try the stuff himself. Now – bending closer to sniff it – he had to try very hard to stop himself licking the spilt blood off the floor.

A light abruptly snapped on in the corridor. His parents were standing there. Both were smiling. 'Smells tasty, doesn't it?' his father said.

CHAPTER 2
THE GIRL

Elias felt his heart race as his parents stepped inside the kitchen. They stood in front of him, their eyes twinkling. 'Don't be afraid,' his mother said. 'We just need to tell you about something.'

'About what?' Elias whispered, backing off.

'About this.' With a hard snap of his neck, his father shook his jaw – and Elias let out a scream as he saw the jaw lengthen.

A pair of gleaming incisors slipped between his father's lips. His mother's teeth were even sharper and longer.

Elias stumbled back, appalled. 'What… what are you?' he gasped.

'What are *you*, I think you should be asking,' came the answer from his father. 'You share our bloodline, after all.'

'I'm not… not… not like that,' Elias murmured, barely able to breathe.

'And yet you wanted to eat this human heart off a dirty kitchen floor, didn't you?' his mother said. She reached down to pick the heart up.

Elias closed his eyes, tried to ignore the craving he felt as he stared at the heart.

'Ask your questions,' said his father. 'By the way, we don't have capes, in case you're wondering.' He and his wife smiled at one another.

Elias pointed shakily at their teeth.

'Oh, these?' muttered his father. 'We only expose our blood teeth for feeding – or killing humans.

Think of a cat showing its claws to a mouse. It's much the same.'

Elias tried to gather his wits. 'Is that what ordinary people are to you, then? Just… just food?'

'To *us*, you mean?' His mother retracted her teeth. 'It's a little more complicated than that, Elias. We live among humans. All vampires are human, in fact, until they reach adolescence. And apart from the teeth, there are no visible differences between us. But our musculature is tougher, and our blood is wildly different – so we stay away from human hospitals to avoid detection.'

Elias instinctively sensed he was being told the truth, but he didn't want to believe it.

'There is no connection with bats,' his father said, flapping his arms with a light, easy laugh. 'We can't fly. Nor read minds. But we do have great strength. Even young vampires do. If you felt like it, Elias, you could already kill a fully grown man with ease.'

'I'm nothing to do with you!' Elias screamed back.

'Then where does your craving come from?' his father asked mildly. 'Don't worry. You'll soon learn to accept all of this, son. And to help with that, we've brought you a little gift to smooth the way.'

A girl around Elias' own age walked into the room. She was tall, with pale brown eyes and wide lips. Her graceful neck showed fully above a plain white dress. Giving him a brief, nervous glance, she hung her head meekly.

'What's she doing here?' Elias demanded.

'Can't you guess?' his mother replied.

'I don't want to guess,' Elias shot back, forcing his eyes away from the girl's neck. 'I want you to tell me about vampires. Tell me everything.'

So they did.

'All across time, we have encouraged humans to think of us as a myth,' his father explained. 'We linked vampires in their minds to imaginary creatures. Things like trolls, werewolves or witches. Many of the medieval witch-finders were actually vampires – a convenient cover for killing.'

Elias's mind felt numb with fear. 'What about wooden stakes, silver bullets and… um… sunlight?'

'More myths,' his father chuckled. 'More things to make us seem less real.'

Elias thought hard. 'Why kill people? Can't you survive on animal blood?'

'Yes – if we must,' his father answered. 'For a short period of time. But there are consequences to prolonged drinking of non-human blood. Health issues.'

Elias kept finding his eyes darting back to the girl. His parents had left her standing at the back of the room. 'How come vampires have kept their existence a secret for so long?' he asked, tearing his gaze away from her.

'Because there are not many of us,' his father told him. 'And because we are experts at removing marks that might cause suspicion. We never leave, for instance, two puncture marks. Only insane humans do that.' He grinned. 'Plus not many people go missing.'

'Why not?' Elias asked.

'Let's see if you can work that out for yourself,' his father challenged him back.

Elias had no idea what that meant. 'Do you have everlasting life?'

'No. But triple the human span.'

Elias swallowed. Where were the parents he'd known his whole life? He felt nothing in common with the man and woman in front of him – if that's what they even were.

'Do you murder them yourself?' he growled. 'The humans, I mean. Or do you get others to do the dirty work for you?'

His mother's grey eyes suddenly glistened. Elias had never seen them look so bright.

'On party nights we do what we like,' she said, with a catch in her breath. 'But other vampires do most of the killing that is purely for food. Often it's done in poorer parts of the world, where such murders are still easier to get away with. The product is shipped as animal meat cargo. There is almost no difference between human meat and pig – and those differences can be masked.'

Elias' lip curled in disgust.

'I see you are sickened by us,' his father said. 'That's because you still think you are human. But you're already changing, son. Soon you'll want to kill humans just as much as we do. And, if we're right about you, you will personally kill so many that no one will be able to clear up the mess you leave behind.'

Elias recoiled from that. 'What do you mean, if you're right about me?'

His father rolled his tongue around his incisors.

'For generations, we have mixed the bloodlines of various families, looking for the right combination … a vampire capable of leading us, of uniting all the world's scattered clans. We – your mother and I – are the end point of that experiment: the strongest, the most gifted. But you, we believe, will be even more special, Elias. We do not quite know what you will be able to do yet, but we believe that you will lead us to glory.'

'Glory? What are you talking about?'

His mother leaned down to run her finger over the blood on the floor. 'Why else do you think we have always kept you here at home, always safe from danger?' she asked quietly, licking her finger.

Elias shuddered. 'Whatever gifts I have,' he said shakily, 'I'll… I'll never use them for you. Never.'

'Really?' His father abruptly leaped to the back of the kitchen, so fast that Elias barely saw him move. Grasping the girl, he thrust the side of her neck towards Elias.

'Here,' he coaxed, 'try it. Trust me, it tastes much better than you think. And the girl doesn't mind giving it. She wants to, in fact. She can't wait. Watch.'

Elias flinched as his father bit into the girl's naked shoulder, but the girl did not react in any way. She simply accepted it. His father made a slit next to her collarbone.

'Go on,' he urged Elias. 'Drink while the cut is still open for you. You've wanted blood, haven't you? Take some. It will all happen so much faster if you do.'

Elias stared at his father, appalled.

His mother pulled the girl towards her. Almost lazily, she attached her mouth to the bite wound.

Stroking the girl's head in a pet-like way, she sipped as casually from her shoulder as a cow grazing on grass.

'Everything will be OK once you give in to the craving, son,' his father said. 'We all resist at first.'

Elias shivered with revulsion, and strode to the door. He couldn't bear to stay in the same room as them for another second. 'You both… disgust me,' he rasped. 'Everything about you disgusts me. I'll never give in to the craving.'

'You might want to think carefully about that decision,' his father said. 'If you don't change your mind, we'll have no choice but to kill you. You're too powerful to be our enemy.'

His mother folded her arms thoughtfully. 'Perhaps you're not what we think you are, after all,' she said. 'Maybe the mixing of blood lines in your case led to a mistake. An abomination. Is that what you are, Elias?'

With that dark warning, his parents swept past him. But Elias was not to be left alone. He found that his parents had taken the girl to his room.

CHAPTER 3
THE SCENT OF BLOOD

Elias sat on his bed in the slanting light of the moon, watching the girl anxiously.

For a while she simply stood with her back to the wall, as if waiting for him to say something. Then she turned her gaze openly on Elias. There was none of the shyness from before.

'You see,' she said, showing him her long bare arms. 'I am full of life and health – no wounds yet, apart from the cut your father gave me.'

Elias rolled his eyes. 'What does that make you? A prize?'

'In a way, yes it does,' she said.

When Elias simply stared at her, she offered her wrist to him.

'Keep away from me!' he shouted.

'OK, OK,' she said, backing off, 'calm down, will you? I'm not going to hurt you. I have been ordered to give you anything you want, though.'

'Anything?'

'Anything.'

'Then sit down and tell me your name.'

She sat on the only chair in the room, and unexpectedly laughed. Elias liked the sound of it. He watched her glossy black hair bounce on her shoulders.

'My name doesn't matter,' she told him. 'Not until I am named by a vampire. Don't you even know that much? If you choose to keep me, *you* will name me. What would you like to call me?'

Elias felt a chill pass through him at such submissiveness. 'What is your real name?' he asked. 'You know,' he said, when she looked confused. 'what your friends call you?'

She shrugged. 'Jess.'

'Then I'll call you that.'

Jess laughed sharply. 'You can call me whatever you want as long as you drink my blood. Stop messing around, Elias. Both our lives are at stake here.'

'What are you talking about?' Elias said.

She made him look at her. 'Your parents are the most powerful of all known vampires. My whole human family line are surrogates to them, and have been for generations. Our only purpose in life is to serve yours, Elias. If one of you refuses us, the life of a surrogate like me is worth nothing. We are slaughtered like cattle.'

'They kill you?' Elias asked, astonished.

'I won't just be killed, Elias. I'll be feasted on and bled dry.'

Elias stared at Jess, and he could see how frightened she was.

'But … but how can I?' he said, hanging his head. 'I daren't drink human blood! You heard what my parents said. You heard what I might become if I do.'

Jess' mouth twisted with emotion. 'I know nothing of such things. Just drink my blood! I am your meal! Drink it!'

She pressed her wrist suddenly up against Elias' mouth.

Horribly, Elias felt something crack in his jaw and push past his tongue. A new tooth.

'No,' he whispered, shuffling back on the bed. 'Stay away from me, Jess. Stay away!'

Later, he asked from the shadows, 'What do the surrogate families get out of their relationship with the vampires?'

'Long life,' Jess told him proudly. 'And we are looked after, taken care of – we only work if we want to. It is a good life.'

Elias breathed deeply. 'Is it now?'

*

Over the next few weeks, Elias' craving became almost unbearable. It nearly killed him not to drink Jess' blood. On his parents' orders, she remained by his side at all times, a blood temptation. One night, when the craving was so bad he could barely stop shaking, Jess lay next to him on the floor and held him with her strong arms.

'They will kill you if you do not start soon,' she told him gently. 'They will kill us both.'

'I can't drink,' he murmured. 'I won't. I… won't.'

'Then we must at least pretend you are,' Jess said. She stood up and walked across to the sink in his room. Taking a metal and plastic connector from an inner pocket, she inserted something into her wrist.

'What are you doing?' Elias gasped as bright red blood splashed into the sink.

'I must take enough to make it look real,' she insisted. 'If I'm not pale and tired they will know. Young vampires always take too much blood.'

Elias watched as Jess bled herself that night and for the next several in a row. It was horrible to see her lose her vitality, but his parents were pleased and left him alone with her.

Elias let Jess sleep in the bed – long, tired sleeps – while he watched the grounds from the window. He knew where all the guards were positioned now. It was a talent that had grown inside him over the past week – an ability to 'detect' not just where his parents were, but the exact location of all the other vampires in the house and surrounding area.

It's their blood I'm smelling, he realised with rising panic. He could even sense vampires at further distances. That Friday and Saturday night he felt them heading to the edges of nearby towns, intending to feed on helpless drunk people. It made him shudder to think about. Whatever he was becoming, he didn't want any part of it.

Tonight though, as always, the stench of vampires was strongest underneath him – in the basement of the house.

Elias had no idea what was down there, but he had to find out.

'Take me with you,' Jess said.

'No, you stay here and sleep,' Elias told her gently. 'You've done enough for me.'

'It's not just you I'm doing this for,' she fired back. 'It won't be long before they find out I've been tricking them. You may be forgiven, but I will not. Maybe there's a way to escape from the basement. It might be our only chance of getting out of this alive.'

CHAPTER 4
THE BASEMENT

Elias let the exhausted Jess lean against his shoulder as he made his way down the three long stone staircases to the basement. He'd never been allowed down here before. Usually at least one guard stood outside the entrance. Tonight, for the first time, Elias' new gift told him that there were none. Almost all the vampires, including his parents, were inside.

'Are you ready?' he asked Jess.

When she nodded he kicked open the basement door.

What he saw inside shocked him into silence. Yes, there were vampires – many of them – but they were outnumbered.

Outnumbered by the humans.

Caged humans. Hundreds pressed together.

The basement was much bigger than Elias had ever realised. It extended deep under the house, a purpose-built series of chambers.

Elias' parents appeared next to one of the cages.

'Do you like what you see?' his father asked.

What Elias saw horrified him. All of the caged prisoners were human children of various ages. Some looked obese and hopeless. Elias could tell at once that they were being fattened to be fed upon. They looked pitiful.

The others – including many adults – were more athletic.

'They're meant to be chased, aren't they?' Elias realised, turning to his father. He tried to look pleased. 'You don't want your prey to be too easy to catch. And this is why so few humans go missing, isn't it? *You breed your own.*'

'Clever boy. Finally, you're understanding. I knew you would.' Elias saw the relief in his father's eyes. 'The breeding humans are elsewhere. But those training for the hunts are all kept here. Do you want to see them?'

Elias kept his voice even. 'Of course.'

He felt Jess dig her frightened nails into him as they were taken down to a gym training arena.

'You didn't know any of this existed?' Elias whispered to her.

'No,' she whispered back, as shocked as him. 'What have they turned these children into?'

Two teenaged girls were locked like wrestlers on the gym floor. They paused their fight when Elias and Jess entered, gazed at them fiercely. *What have they been told about their future?* Elias wondered. *Lies, probably, to make them more compliant.*

His nose twitched. There was a reek of vampires down here – they obviously came to the cellar often, to tend the flock, and take those they wanted from time to time.

One boy in particular drew Elias' attention – a fair-haired, regal-looking older teen in spectacularly good condition. Elias detected the smell of his cousin Anya all around his cage, as if she had been here many times to observe him.

'Do you know what you are being bred for?' Elias suddenly shouted at him.

Surprisingly, the boy answered. 'Yes, to be hunted. But if I escape I get to keep my life.'

'You'll never get beyond the grounds of the house,' Elias told him.

'I will take my chance on that when the hunt comes,' the boy replied.

Seeing his direct, brave stare, Elias felt a surge of emotion shoot through him. He felt more in his heart for this one human boy and for Jess tiredly leaning against his side than for any of the vampires in this place.

As Elias left the basement, one of the fattened children begged for his help.

'Please, sir. Please, sir….'

The boy flopped to the front of his cage. His legs were too weak to stand, and the vampire minders laughed at his attempts to get up.

Elias laughed with them, but secretly he hated the vampires more than ever.

*

'What can we do for them?' Jess asked him in despair that evening, when they were alone together in his room again.

'I don't know,' Elias answered hollowly. He felt powerless. 'I just don't know.'

A little later his father knocked on his bedroom door. Jess quickly pressed her neck against Elias' mouth.

'Good, good.' His father nodded, his own teeth briefly showing, when he saw Elias apparently feeding. 'I see you are nearly ready. After tonight, you will be fully so.'

Elias frowned. 'Why? What happens tonight?'

'The Great Hunt. Your coming-of-age party, son. When you see what a real vampire can do, your last doubts will disappear. Come and join the rest of the family. We're gathering downstairs.'

CHAPTER 5
THE GREAT HUNT

Elias had never seen so many of his family in one place. Uncles, aunts, cousins and nieces all milled excitedly on the ground floor of the house, snuffling like dogs, sniffing the air. Some were already baring their teeth.

'At last, we can be ourselves around him!' Uncle Bart exclaimed, and a huge roar of laughter went up.

'What about the girl?' his nephew Roger bellowed good-naturedly. 'Are we sharing her, Elias?'

'No, we are not,' Elias answered – and his voice had a power he'd never heard in it before. It was deeper, full of threat.

'Well said!' his father called out to Elias. Then he gazed around the suddenly quiet room. 'You heard him! Does anyone doubt any longer what I told you about Elias? My son will lead us. I told you he would!'

*

Elias, with Jess beside him, was driven to the hunting area in the family limousine. A black Daimler carrying his parents and a couple of guards cruised behind, along with the rest of the family in their own vehicles.

Nearly an hour later they parked in a deserted area of beach on the south coast.

Elias could sense all the vampires for miles around. It was the biggest concentration he'd ever known. Dozens, all excitedly waiting. Too many to escape from. If there was going to be a chance to get away, it would have to come later.

Anya, a cousin on his mother's side he'd never liked, walked softly up to Elias. Without breaking the skin, she sank her teeth into his neck.

'Don't get any ideas,' she whispered. 'Your father may believe in you, but I'm not so sure you're one of us.'

Elias shrugged her off as a huge lorry rattled into view. A metal cage was lowered from it, one of those Elias had seen in the basement.

Elias recognised the boy inside at once.

'He's mine, not yours,' Anya warned Elias – and unfurled her fangs. Seeing that, all the vampires whooped and shouted their approval. They dragged the cage door open.

For a moment the boy inside gazed up and around him with an open mouth. *He's not looking at the vampires*, Elias realised. *He's looking at the sky. They never let him out, did they? He's never seen it before.*

A look of pure, beautiful astonishment briefly filled the boy's face.

Then, with one hard glance at Elias – and a defiant thumbing of his nose at Anya – the boy ran off into the night.

Within seconds the darkness swallowed him up.

Anya let him go. She inspected her nails. She chatted idly to a friend – someone Elias had never met. Then, as if she had all the time in the world, she yawned and quietly lowered her body into a crouch.

Next second, with an animal's grunt, she was off, low to the ground, sniffing – after him.

Everyone waited expectantly. The night remained velvety dark and quiet. Then… a scream like nothing Elias had ever heard before, and from the gloom Anya reappeared, dragging the boy with her.

'Oh God,' Jess murmured, and Elias could hardly bear to look either because Anya had twisted and turned the boy's body almost inside out. Her mouth was still attached to the boy's lifeless neck. She only lifted her teeth away from his flesh to warn off two adolescent vampires who tried to snatch him off her.

With the boy still dangling from her mouth, Anya was carried by two adult vampires back to a van to finish her meal in peace.

And then the real hunt began.

Jubilant vampires across the beach all shouted impatiently as a much bigger lorry pulled up. From the back, 12 crated children and 6 adults were released onto the sands.

'Party time!' one vampire yelled, and a huge laugh went up from the rest of them.

The prisoners stood dumbly, blinking about them for a moment, just as the boy had done. *Run, run, run*, Elias secretly urged, and within seconds they shook themselves.

Sprinting, they headed fast for the sand dunes and scrub grass. Could they make it to town? When Elias glanced up, the nearest lights were a faint line of impossibly distant orange on the horizon.

Half the vampires gleefully went after the humans. They included Elias' father. Tearing off his shirt, he was suddenly muscular and frightening as he chased down a heavy man and killed him.

One by one the humans were hunted to a standstill, until only a single man remained. He was the largest man of all – huge and incredibly tough. Surrounded by three teen vampires, he silently fought off their ferocious attacks for nearly a minute. Then, in desperation, Elias saw him raise his head and call out to Elias' father.

'This is not what you promised us!' he yelled. 'You promised we would have a chance! You gave us your word!'

Unexpectedly, it was his mother who responded.

She walked back to the lorry. Strolled back to the man. Handed him a knife.

'Do you need any other weapons?' she asked him.

'What? Against you?' the man asked. Enormous next to Elias' slim mother, it looked like a totally unequal match.

And it was. Before he could even raise the knife, she easily disarmed him, and then… then she was on him. Sinking her teeth into his neck, she hung under him, choking his windpipe, riding him like a hound. The man did everything he could to tear her off, but she was like a leech on his throat, stuck fast, and finally even the bull-like man staggered and fell to his knees.

As soon as he did so, Elias' father was the first to join in the feeding frenzy. Six other vampires from his family tore the man apart.

Seeing the killing, all that blood, Elias felt… something happen to him.

The craving!

It suddenly burst through him. *No*, he thought – but he couldn't ignore it. It was beyond his control. He, too, desperately wanted blood.

'No, please,' Jess whispered, seeing his eyes, but Elias barely heard her.

He staggered across the sand.

All the other vampires respectfully moved aside as he looked down at the man's body. 'Go on,' whispered his father, 'we left some for you.'

Elias bent over the man. Everything – every single part of his body – demanded blood.

Then he stopped. Gazing down, he saw the huge man's face screwed up in its final agonies.

No, Elias thought. He brought his head back up. Felt the wind off the sea brush across his hair. *No. I won't.*

'I told you!' came a scream from a nearby van.

Anya staggered from it, her face bloated with blood. 'He is an abomination!' she shrieked. 'No true vampire could resist this feast!'

There was silence for a moment. Then Elias saw his parents' faces harden, and together they nodded.

Seconds later, he and Jess were driven home and thrown onto the hallway floor. Elias' mother loomed over his face. She carefully smelt his mouth. 'So, you have not been drinking human blood, after all,' she said. 'Hold them both down,' she ordered, and Anya and a few others did so.

A vein was quickly opened in Jess' wrist and a whole jug's worth of blood withdrawn.

Elias' own father held his mouth open, forcing him to swallow, to drink it. He couldn't stop them.

He drank and drank, and then he passed out.

CHAPTER 6
DESTINY

Elias woke on the floor of his bedroom, with Jess beside him. She was holding his face in her hands. He could feel the shudders of her sobs. He turned to face her. Kissed her.

'You're going to transform into *their* horrible vampire now, aren't you?' she whispered. 'I'm sure that's why they left me in here with you – to become your first real meal.'

'I don't know,' Elias murmured. 'I really don't know, Jess. I tried. I –'

'I know.' She placed her fingers softly across his lips. 'I know you did. Let's just lie here for a while together, for the little time you have left to be human.'

They held each other. All night they held each other, and at every moment Elias expected to turn into something terrifying that attacked Jess. He sensed it would happen very soon. The craving was worse than ever.

But when dawn arrived and Elias was still human, his father came to see him. He examined Elias roughly, pushing aside his tongue to look at his teeth. There was no compassion left in his eyes. 'You are not what I thought you were,' he said finally. 'I do not know what you are, but you are not one of us.'

'What happens now?' Elias asked him.

'I think you know,' his father answered.

*

All morning Elias was held under guard with Jess. Outside, they could both hear indistinct raised voices and the sound of something being built in the grounds.

Just after midday his parents both came to visit him. Elias could see the bitter disappointment in their eyes. And their fear. To them, *he* was the monster.

In the grounds outside, vampires gathered.

'They are waiting,' his mother told Elias.

'For my death?'

'For your execution,' she corrected him.

'Will it be quick?' he murmured.

'No,' she told him. 'There's no chance of that.'

'I don't mean for me.' Elias gazed into his mother's eyes. 'I mean for Jess.'

'No,' she replied loudly enough for both him and Jess to hear clearly. 'For Jess' crime there is only one fate. After you are dead, a dozen will feed on her at once.'

*

His parents left. Shortly after, three of his cousins bound Elias tightly with ropes. Then, along with Jess, he was carried into the house grounds.

Vampires lined the lawn, a crowd baying for his death. Elias could smell them all. He suddenly realised that. He could smell *all vampires everywhere*. Not just those at the house and in nearby towns and cities. He could detect vampires wherever they were in the world. Despite the utter horror of his position, it was an intoxicating moment.

As Jess was wrenched from his side, Elias snatched a kiss from her.

She was taken away and tied to a wooden post. Elias looked for the only victory for them both he could take to the grave, and managed to shout out her name, praising her.

Jess caught his eye. 'I love you,' she mouthed.

The execution ceremony began.

Elias' father took the lead. He called on all the vampires in his family to feed upon Elias at the same time.

Forward they shuffled towards him – aunts, uncles, distant relatives Elias hadn't seen since he was a child. Anya led them, smiling, her teeth already bared.

Elias readied himself.

His arms and legs were spread apart, and his family knelt all around him, waiting for his father to give the order.

Elias took a moment to look up. Beyond the faces

of his family he could see a sunny, blue sky. A single tiny white cloud hovered near the sun.

The next moment he heard his father say, '*Now.*'

All the vampires dropped their mouths towards Elias. With them so close, Elias gasped. The craving! It wasn't just a thirst any longer. It suddenly rose like an unstoppable force inside Elias...

... and blasted out of him.

Whatever it was, Elias instantly found the strength to break the rope holding his shoulders down.

Anya was closest to him. Twisting his head, Elias chose her neck and bit into the softest part of it.

The taste!

As soon as the first drop of her vampire blood shot into his veins, Elias knew what his true destiny was. He knew what to do. Knew what he was.

Not the leader of the vampires.

The opposite.

All their experiments in mixing bloodlines had
gone wrong.

He was all their worst dreams rolled into one. He
was their nightmare. Their scourge.

His destiny was not to lead the vampires, but to
fight them.

As Elias looked around him, with that first taste
of vampire blood still in his mouth, he could
sense them all, knew where they were hiding.

'*I see you,*' he whispered.

Hearing that, the nearest vampires to Elias shrank
back in awe and fear.

That fear redoubled as he rose up from the slab
they had lain him on. Snapping the rest of his

ropes, he rose not just to his feet but into the air, beyond their touch.

Within seconds he freed Jess. The vampires tried to stop him, but he just shrugged them off. Even combined they could not hold him, and some part of them knew that.

Once Jess was in a safe place, Elias turned back to the vampires. His teeth grew. So did the knuckles of his hands. Sharp bones broke the skin. Elias stared down, marvelling at the claws. *Weapons*, he thought, realising that there were others to come, things about himself he would not discover now, but later.

Humanity had finally found its champion against the vampires.

ABOUT THE AUTHOR

Cliff McNish is acclaimed as 'one of our
most talented thriller writers' (*The Times*).
His debut fantasy series, *The Doomspell Trilogy*,
saw him hailed as 'a great new voice in writing
for children' (*The Bookseller*), and he has been
published in 26 languages worldwide. His
multiple award winning novel *Breathe: A Ghost
Story* was voted in April 2013 as one of the
top 100 adult and children's novels of all
time by the Schools Library Network.